PSALMS

Rose Visual
Bible Studies

Psalms
Rose Visual Bible Studies

© 2023 Rose Publishing

Published by Rose Publishing
An imprint of Tyndale House Ministries
Carol Stream, Illinois
www.hendricksonrose.com

ISBN 978-1-4964-7981-5

Author: Titus O'Bryant, ThM, Senior Pastor, LifePoint Church, Reisterstown, Maryland

Scriptures taken from the Holy Bible, New International Version®, NIV®. Copyright © 1973, 1978, 1984, 2011 by Biblica, Inc.™ Used by permission of Zondervan. All rights reserved worldwide. www.zondervan.com The "NIV" and "New International Version" are trademarks registered in the United States Patent and Trademark Office by Biblica, Inc.™

Scripture quotations marked NLT are taken from the Holy Bible, New Living Translation, copyright ©1996, 2004, 2015 by Tyndale House Foundation. Used by permission of Tyndale House Publishers, Carol Stream, Illinois 60188. All rights reserved.

Scripture quotations marked ESV are from the ESV® Bible (The Holy Bible, English Standard Version®), copyright © 2001 by Crossway, a publishing ministry of Good News Publishers. Used by permission. All rights reserved. The ESV text may not be quoted in any publication made available to the public by a Creative Commons license. The ESV may not be translated in whole or in part into any other language.

Images used under license from Shutterstock.com: Dmitri Fedorov, cover; Freedom Studio, p. 3, 7; Anton Jankovoy, p. 3, 23, 24, 36; Fabio Lamanna, p. 3, 37; onneur, p. 3, 53; CJRomano, p. 3, 67, 83; Foxartbox, p. 3; Chat Karen Studio, p. 3, 97; Sean Xu, p. 5; Creative Travel Projects, p. 6, 8, 22; Deer worawut, p. 9; Physics_joe, p. 25; I'm from Ukraine, p. 30; Kelly vanDellen, p. 38, 52; Peter Kolejak, p. 39; Africa Studio, p. 41; Renata Sedmakova, p. 45; Golden Gate of the Temple Mount (Jerusalem, March 8, 2023) Nick Brundle Photography, p. 46; Azer Mess, p. 54, 66; SantaLiza, p. 55; Amanita Silvicora, (crown), Incomible (cross), Eduard Radu (scroll), p. 58; Worawee Meepian, p. 61; John Theodor, p. 68, 82; Mariusz Niedzwiedzki, p. 69; Cortyn, p. 71; Daniel Chetroni, p. 84; Poidl, p. 85; IoanaB, p. 88; Sherry Talbot, p. 90; Tatevosian Yana, p. 92; Maxwell Photography, p. 98; Amenic181, p. 101; Keep Smiling Photography, p. 103; Happy Art, icons (book, lightbulb, compass, plant). Smithsonian images: David playing the harp, National Museum of African Art (gift of Joseph and Patricia Brumit), p. 15; Henry Wadsworth Longfellow, National Portrait Gallery (gift of Forrest H. Kennedy), p. 47. Library of Congress images: Horatio Gates Spafford, Jerusalem, Garabed Krikorian (1885), p. 17; "Fountain of Siloam Valley of Jehosophat," David Roberts (1842), p. 72. Images from Unsplash: Timothy Eberly, p. 16.

Printed in the United States of America
010423VP

Contents

"May these words of my mouth and this meditation of my heart be pleasing in your sight, LORD, my Rock and my Redeemer."

Psalm 19:14

Psalms

Not long ago, I had an opportunity to take a drive through part of the Appalachian Mountains in southwest Virginia. My road was the Blue Ridge Parkway, a historic highway winding through beautiful peaks and valleys. From the isolation and safety of my car, I observed through the windows tall trees, grazing deer, and views overlooking broad valleys.

After my scenic drive, I parked my car at the base of Sharp Top Mountain, one of Virginia's tallest peaks. That's when my adventure really began. Once the barrier of my car was removed, I was able to hear, see, touch, and feel the wild beauty surrounding me: hawks circling the sky while scanning for prey, the strong scent of the forest trees, and the roll of thunder from an approaching storm. I hiked all the way to the top of the mountain that summer day. My muscles ached and my body became tired, but my experience of the mountain was far grander than only observing it from behind my car windows. A wide gap stretches between observing and experiencing the wild beauty of the natural world.

The book of Psalms records for us the shared history of those who have not only observed but *experienced* God. These are the songs of God-followers who have crested the summits and languished in the valleys of life while raising their voices to praise or complain to

God. Their experience is not safe or sanitary, but their songs are wild and free, beautiful and true.

This study is your invitation to step out of safety and into the wild beauty that comes from experiencing God, as you go deeper in your relationship with him through the psalms. Over the next six sessions, you will have an opportunity to immerse yourself in different types of prayer-songs from the book of Psalms, consider the background of the psalms and their connections with Jesus, and explore how the songs you sing and the song of your life reflect themes in the book of Psalms.

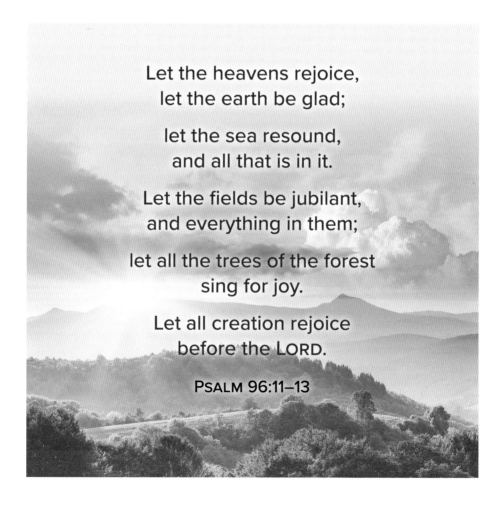

Let the heavens rejoice,
let the earth be glad;

let the sea resound,
and all that is in it.

Let the fields be jubilant,
and everything in them;

let all the trees of the forest
sing for joy.

Let all creation rejoice
before the LORD.

PSALM 96:11–13

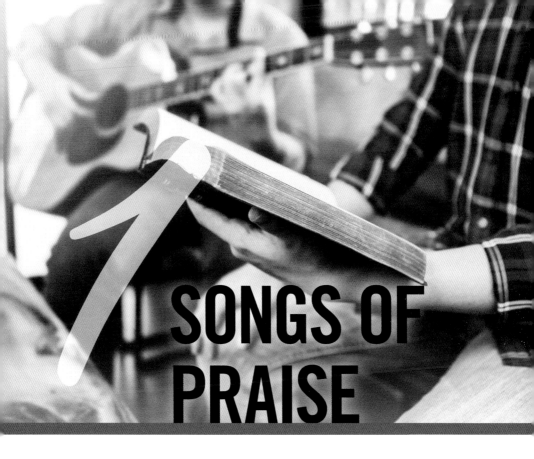

SONGS OF PRAISE

Psalms 1 and 150

Songs of Praise

"That person is like a tree planted by streams of water." PSALM 1:3

We become like whatever we choose to worship, and the connection between our worship and our faith cannot be overstated. The words, symbols, and actions that express our worship shape our faith and character. If we worship wealth or leisure, then we are likely to become increasingly greedy or lazy. If we worship the living God, he will graciously shape our character to match his over time. If our worship is shallow, then our faith will lack deep roots that can make us strong and productive throughout every season of life. But if our worship focuses on God's character and faithfulness while expressing the full range of the human experience—our successes and shortcomings; our great joys and terrible griefs—then our faith will grow to become unshakable, and our lives will be rich, full, and steady.

Whether chanted in a synagogue, sung from a hymnal, or read from projectors on walls— the psalms have provided God's people with prayers, poetry, imagery, and themes that defined both worship and faith for many generations. By studying, praying, and living the psalms, our lives become an enduring song of praise to the Lord and grow like a strong, well-watered fruitful tree that thrives through every season.

Key Psalms to Read

For this session, read Psalms 1 and 150, the first and last psalms in the book.

Optional Reading

Jesus knew and sang the psalms. Consider how worshiping with the psalms might have influenced his teaching in passages like Matthew 6:9–13, the Lord's Prayer.

> "Let everything that has breath praise the LORD."
>
> **PSALM 150:6**

Know It

1. In what ways are the righteous and the wicked contrasted in Psalm 1?

THE RIGHTEOUS ARE ...	THE WICKED ARE ...

2. What is the dominant theme in Psalm 150, the book's closing psalm?

3. Why do you think these two specific psalms were placed first and last in the book of Psalms?

The Five Books of Psalms

The psalms are divided into five large sections or "books." Each book concludes with a doxology—a short, memorable expression of praise.

SECTION	PSALMS	DOXOLOGY
Book 1	1–41	"Praise be to the Lord, the God of Israel, from everlasting to everlasting. Amen and Amen" (Ps. 41:13).
Book 2	42–72	"Praise be to his glorious name forever; may the whole earth be filled with his glory. Amen and Amen" (Ps. 72:19).
Book 3	73–89	"Praise be to the Lord forever! Amen and Amen" (Ps. 89:52).
Book 4	90–106	"Praise be to the Lord, the God of Israel, from everlasting to everlasting. Let all the people say, 'Amen!' Praise the Lord" (Ps. 106:48).
Book 5	107–150	"Praise the Lord.... Let everything that has breath praise the Lord. Praise the Lord" (Ps. 150:1, 6; In fact, all of Psalm 150 functions as a doxology).

Notice how books one, two, and three each conclude with the words "Amen and Amen." Book four ends with "Amen! Praise the Lord" or more literally "Amen! Hallelujah." Book five closes the entire collection with a final "Praise the Lord" or "Hallelujah."

Psalm Writers

The book of Psalms had many authors and it developed gradually throughout Israel's history. Moses may have been the first author of Hebrew poetry. In Exodus 15, Moses composes a song praising God for Israel's escape from Egypt and rescue at the Red Sea, sometime in the fifteenth century BC. Many of the psalms are attributed to King David who reigned around 1000 BC. The book of Psalms probably did not reach its final form until about 450 BC, as Ezra and his colleague scribes completed their compilation and editing work after returning home to Israel from exile in Babylon and Persia. Psalms like 137 were probably written during the time of Israel's captivity and exile.

The book of Psalms identifies several authors but leaves about a third of the psalms unattributed:

- 73 psalms by David
- 49 psalms are unattributed
- 12 psalms by Asaph
- 11 psalms by the sons of Korah
- 2 psalms by King Solomon
- 1 psalm by Moses
- 1 psalm by Ethan
- 1 psalm by Heman

Hebrew and English Scriptures

While the Hebrew Scriptures and English translations of the Old Testament contain the same books of the Bible, they appear in different divisions and order. English translations follow the organization and book order of the Latin Vulgate, which was translated from Hebrew manuscripts into Latin by Jerome in the fourth century. The order of books in the Hebrew Bible places the book of Psalms near the end, rather than in the middle, like most English translations.

The divisions of the Hebrew Bible are:

- **Torah (Law):** Genesis, Exodus, Leviticus, Numbers, and Deuteronomy—the five books of Moses;

- **Nevi'im (Prophets):** Former Prophets: Joshua, Judges, Samuel, Kings; and Latter Prophets: Isaiah, Jeremiah, Ezekiel, and concluding with the twelve minor prophets; and

- **Ketuvim (Writings):** Psalms, Proverbs, Job, Song of Songs, Ruth, Lamentations, Ecclesiastes, Esther, Daniel, Ezra and Nehemiah, and Chronicles. (Some scroll collections offer alternative book order for the Ketuvim.)

The entire collection of books is referred to as the Tanakh, which is a combination of the names for the sections: Torah, Nevi'im, and Ketuvim.

The Book of Psalms

The English title *Psalms* comes from the title used in the Septuagint, which is the Greek translation of the Old Testament. In the Septuagint, the Greek word *psalmos* was used to translate the Hebrew word *mizmor*, which may mean "song." The Hebrew title for the book of Psalms is *Tehillim*, which means "praises."

The Psalms Scroll of the Dead Sea Scrolls (c. AD 30–50)

Hallelujah

Hallelujah! This single word is formed by combining two Hebrew words: *hallel* and *Yahweh*.

- *Hallel* simply means "to praise," and it is used in various places throughout the Old Testament.

- *Yahweh* is the personal name for God revealed to Moses in Exodus 3–6.

Some English Bible translations keep the word as *hallelujah*, while many others translate its meaning: "Praise the LORD."

Hallelujah did not appear to be used until around 600 BC during the time that Israel experienced defeat from foreign enemies and exile from their homeland. The word first appears in the Bible in Psalm 104:35 and then frequently through the end of the book of Psalms, though it appears nowhere else in the Old Testament. *Hallelujah* is used twenty-three times and is, in fact, the very last word of the book of Psalms (Ps. 150:6).

Amen

The Hebrew word *amen* is a way of saying "let it be," "surely," or "truly." This word is related to the Hebrew word *aman,* which means "to believe," "to trust," or "to have faith." *Amen* is used to affirm something believed or stated as true. In the Old Testament, this word is often used to emphasize blessings and curses (for example, Deut. 27:15–26; Jer. 11:5). In the New Testament, the Greek translation of *amen* serves as the final word in the Bible: "The grace of the Lord Jesus be with God's people. Amen" (Rev. 22:21).

Christians adopted the word *hallelujah* and carried it over directly from Hebrew to Greek in the early church. In English, the word can be spelled *alleluia* or *hallelujah*. In Revelation 19, the word is repeated four times in a song of praise to God. This indicates how the early church employed the word in their worship. When we pray or praise God using this word, we are joining our voices with believers who have used the same expression of praise for more than 2,000 years.

King David playing the harp; a page from a 15th-century Ethiopian Psalter

The Language of Prayer

Infants learn how to speak by hearing and then mimicking sounds from their parents. Christians can learn how to speak with God by hearing, internalizing, and then mirroring the thoughts, words, and characteristics seen in the book of Psalms.

In many parts of the modern church, a growing separation between worship and prayer has emerged, as worship became more closely associated with a style of music and with musical performance. But for much of church history, prayer and worship have been synonymous. The psalms reflect this unity between prayer and worship.

In Luke's account of the Lord's Prayer, the disciples come to Jesus and ask, "Lord, teach us to pray" (Luke 11:1). The language that Jesus used in prayer is the language of the psalms. Jesus's model for prayer echoes themes found in the psalms (Matt. 6:9–13; Luke 11:2–4). The sixteenth-century Reformer Martin Luther incorporated the psalms into his prayer life, explaining: "The Lord's Prayer is my prayer, I use it, and intermingle at times something from the Psalms."

The psalms are worship-prayer songs lifted up to God. Through reading, meditating on, discussing, and praying through the psalms, we learn the language of prayer and communion with God. The psalms teach us how to speak with God about his person, kingdom, and will as we approach him with our daily needs, our debts and failures, and our temptations and trials.

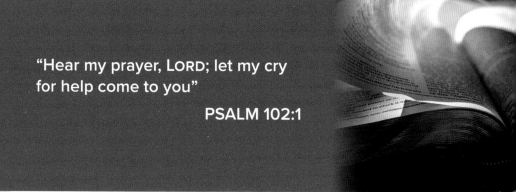

"Hear my prayer, LORD; let my cry for help come to you"

PSALM 102:1

It Is Well With My Soul

Horatio Spafford was a man who knew the unfairness of life. He was a prominent Chicago lawyer and businessman. Early in his career, he worked for the abolition of slavery.

By the 1870s, he was married with four daughters, and he was a supporter and friend of the evangelist D. L. Moody. Then, the great Chicago fire of 1871 devastated Spafford's business interests by destroying his real estate investments along the shore of Lake Michigan.

Just two years later, he sent his wife and daughters (ages eleven, nine, five, and two) to England on a ship. He planned to join them soon for a vacation and to be part of Moody's campaigns later that year. On the voyage, an iron vessel tore through the steamer crossing the Atlantic. The ship sank in just twelve minutes time. Two hundred and twenty-six passengers lost their lives and eighty-one were rescued. Mrs. Spafford was recovered alive, but unconscious, floating on the wreckage. Her four daughters were gone.

She soon telegrammed her husband, "Saved Alone, What shall I do?"

Horatio immediately took a ship to join his wife, and on the crossing, he wrote these words:

> *When peace like a river, attendeth my way,*
> *When sorrows like sea billows roll;*
> *Whatever my lot, Thou hast taught me to say,*
> *It is well, it is well with my soul.*

Now that is true worship in the face of adversity and grief. Horatio and his wife continued living lives of worship, and in several years moved to Israel and began a ministry reaching out to serve and demonstrate love to Muslims, Jews, and Christians.

Life Application Questions

1. When you hear the words *praise* and *worship,* what comes to mind? What do praise and worship mean to you in your life?

2. In Psalm 150:2, the Lord is to be praised for his "acts of power" and his "surpassing greatness." What are some of God's acts of power and greatness that inspire you to worship?

3. How can we continue to worship the Lord during times of grief, illness, loneliness, and disappointment? What might worship look like and feel like in those seasons of life?

4. In Psalm 150, musical instruments in the hands of musicians are celebrated. But worship is not limited to music. What "instruments" (musical or not) has God placed in your hands that you could use to praise him?

5. Read Psalm 1:3. What are some practical ways you could become more grounded and flourish in your spiritual life?

6. Find an outdoor spot with a tree. Take some time to consider the tree's unseen roots, the visible trunk and branches, the changes it experiences through seasons, and its life cycle. What conclusions can you draw about your life of faith and the life of a tree?

Your Song

Compose your own prayer-song from Psalm 150 to match your life and express you heart to God.

Praise the Lord ...

_____

_____

_____

_____

_____

_____

_____

_____

_____

_____

_____

Notes

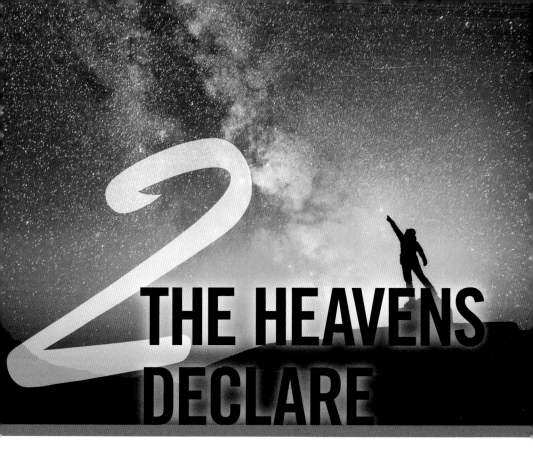

THE HEAVENS
DECLARE

Psalm 19 and 119

The Heavens Declare

*"They have no speech, they use no words ...
yet their voice goes out into all the earth."*
PSALM 19:3–4

Every movement creates waves. We can't see
them, but anytime something physical moves,
sound waves are created. These waves travel
through space, atmosphere, and objects.
Energy creates movement and sound—even
when we don't hear those sounds.

In our neighborhood of the Milky Way Galaxy,
the biggest most energetic force generating the
greatest amount of movement is our sun. The
sun is in constant motion, creating vibrations
or waves of sound. We see the light from the
sun (or rather we see *because of* its light),
and we enjoy its warmth, but we can't hear
its sound ... well, not until recently. NASA
researchers have found a way to record the
sound waves generated by the sun and then
scale them up to an audible human hearing
range. The sun is singing a song![1]

Every human movement creates vibrations,
or waves. Every action, every word, every
thought—whether hidden away or visible,
public or private—is forming a song. By
following the Lord's instructions through his
Word, our life joins nature's song of praise to
him. May our words and thoughts be pleasing
to the Lord, our rock and redeemer (Ps. 19:14).

Read It

Key Psalms to Read

For this session, read Psalms 19 and 119:105–112.

Optional Reading

Read 2 Peter 1:12–21, which helps us understand how God has spoken to us over time in writings from prophets and poets, as well as apostles, and most clearly through the person of Jesus Christ.

You may also want to take time to read all of Psalm 119, the longest psalm in the book.

"The heavens declare the glory of God; the skies proclaim the work of his hands."

PSALM 19:1

Know It

1. In Psalm 19, what are the different ways that God communicates with us?

2. Psalm 19:7–9 uses parallelism to express the majesty of God's Word. What are the six terms and descriptions used? (The first one is done for you.)

   1. _____The Law_____ of the Lord is _____perfect_____ .

   2. _____ of the Lord are _____ .

   3. _____ of the Lord are _____ .

   4. _____ of the Lord are _____ .

   5. _____ of the Lord is _____ .

   6. _____ of the Lord are _____ .

3. In Psalm 119:105–112, how does God's Word act as a light through different life experiences?

Types of Psalms

Over the years, there have been many attempts to classify the psalms according to their main themes and their intended uses as personal or public (communal) expressions. Though every classification system seems to fall just a bit short in its attempt to classify each and every psalm, looking at the different types of psalms can help us understand them better.

In the 1920s and 1930s, Hermann Gunkel created a framework to categorize the psalms according to their forms which he identified as:

- **hymns:** praise that describes and focuses on God's character;

- **communal laments:** national expressions of pain and calamity;

- **individual laments:** personal expressions of pain and distress;

- **individual thanksgiving:** praise for God's specific actions in a psalmist's personal life; and

- **royal songs:** praise focusing on the promised Messiah or celebrating the King of Israel or God as King over all.[2]

Psalms 19 and 119 can both be classified as songs of praise. They reveal God's wisdom, so they are often also considered wisdom songs or prayers.

Many subcategories could be placed within these main categories, such as psalms of confession, cursing, wisdom, Zion or Jerusalem, and pilgrimage, among others.

In the mid-twentieth century, Claus Westermann simplified the psalms' classifications into two broad categories: praise and lament.[3] While unique personal matters (forgiveness, betrayal, hardship, thanksgiving) and national themes (pilgrimage to Jerusalem, defeat and exile, threats from enemies) are explored through the psalms, the overarching categories of lament and praise help us make sense of individual songs and include them in our own lives and worship.

Of special interest in identifying these forms is a technical term: *Sitz im Leben*. That's German for "situation in life." What was the particular situation in life for the nation or for the author that informs the content of a specific psalm? While we don't know precisely the situations that gave rise to every psalm, some of the occasions for writing or use of the psalms are very clear, and these include:

- traveling to Jerusalem for worship (Ps. 120–134),

- mourning in exile from the homeland (Ps. 137), and

- seeking forgiveness of sin (Ps. 51).

General and Special Revelation

God reveals who he is through general and special revelation (or revealing). In Psalm 19, we discover both general and special revelation, from the majesty of God's created world in verses 1–6 to the supreme value of God's Word in verses 7–13.

What is general revelation?

General revelation is available to everyone. The wonder and beauty of the heavens and the earth demonstrate God's glory, power, and creative presence. Standing at the base or pinnacle of a majestic mountain, gazing at a blanket of stars filling the night sky, or hearing and feeling the power of the ocean can inspire a sense of awe and wonder that reminds anyone that there must be something greater than us who caused it all. General revelation is a common grace that teaches us about God's presence.

"The heavens declare the glory of God; the skies proclaim the work of his hands. Day after day they pour forth speech; night after night they reveal knowledge" (Ps. 19:1–2).

What is special revelation?

Special revelation is a specific message from God. The Bible, from beginning to end, is a record of God's special revealing of himself to his people. God most clearly taught us about his own character by entering our reality when the eternal Son of God was born and lived and died and rose again. All of Scripture points to Jesus Christ as the clearest revelation of God to humanity.

"The decrees of the Lord are firm, and all of them are righteous" (Ps. 19:9).

GENERAL REVELATION	SPECIAL REVELATION
God reveals who he is through the created world, history, and the inner being of all humans.	God reveals who he is to particular people at specific times through divine speech, Scripture, prophets, and the incarnation of Christ.

Related to the special revelation of Scripture are two other important terms to know: inspiration and illumination.

- Inspiration is more than creativity and brilliance when it comes to the words of the Bible. Inspiration refers to the process that God used to write and record the words of Scripture that serve as a witness to God himself. The Holy Spirit of God used the unique vocabulary, culture, and life experience of more than forty different authors to write the texts making up the Bible (see 2 Peter 1:19–21; 2 Tim. 3:16–17).

- Illumination describes what happens as we read, study, and meditate on God's Word. The Holy Spirit takes the Word of God and helps us apply it to our lives. We find comfort, guidance, correction, and instruction for life as we understand God's message to us (see 2 Cor. 3:15–17; James 1:22–25).

Great Is Thy Faithfulness

Thomas Chisholm (1866–1960) lived a remarkable but common life for his time. He was a schoolteacher, a newspaper publisher, a pastor, and an insurance salesman. He faced poor health all throughout his life, causing him to lose jobs along the way and struggle to support his family. But his passion for expressing his relationship with God through his writing remained constant. It's said that he wrote more than 1,200 poems over his lifetime.

In his late fifties, he mailed a collection of his poems to a man named William Runyan who was compiling a hymnal. Runyan was facing his own struggles at the time. After twenty years of being a pastor and traveling evangelist, Runyan was forced to step down because he was going deaf. The lyrics of one of Chisholm's poems caught Runyan's attention, and he put the words to music to create the song, "Great Is Thy Faithfulness." This hymn became popular during the Depression Era and later a favorite at Billy Graham evangelism crusades, making it one of the most beloved hymns of the twentieth century.

> Great is Thy faithfulness, O God my Father,
> There is no shadow of turning with Thee.
> Thou changest not, Thy compassions, they fail not;
> As Thou hast been, Thou forever will be.
>
> Great is Thy faithfulness!
> Great is Thy faithfulness!
> Morning by morning new mercies I see;
> All I have needed Thy hand hath provided.
> Great is Thy faithfulness, Lord, unto me!

Summer and winter and springtime and harvest,
Sun, moon and stars in their courses above
Join with all nature in manifold witness
To Thy great faithfulness, mercy and love.

If you feel stuck in a monotonous routine or are experiencing significant change; if you are on top of the world or if you're carrying the weight of the world on your shoulders, remember that God is *always* faithful.

Life Application Questions

1. How much understanding of God can humans glean from general revelation alone?

2. Where do you see God's glory, power, faithfulness, and beauty displayed in the created world?

3. When has God's Word been a "light on [your] path" (Ps. 119:105), guiding you through a difficult season or decision?

4. How are you looking to God's Word to guide you today?

5. Who has positively influenced your life and faith? Who are you intentionally influencing toward faithfulness?

6. When you have an opportunity, quietly observe a sunrise or sunset. Contemplate how the regularity of the sun reminds you of the faithfulness of God. How have you personally experienced God's faithful love?

Your Song

Compose your own prayer-song from Psalm 19 to match your life and express you heart to God.

The heavens declare ...

_____

_____

_____

_____

_____

_____

_____

_____

_____

_____

_____

Notes

3
IN DARKEST VALLEYS

Psalms 22, 23, and 24

In Darkest Valleys

"Even though I walk through the darkest valley, I will fear no evil, for you are with me." PSALM 23:4

Lament and praise are the two poles that balance the book of Psalms. Lament psalms present complaints to God and often pleas for him to intervene in some way. Laments usually still include notes of praise and expressions of trust in the Lord, but lament psalms feel different than purely praise songs. Psalms of praise simply and beautifully worship God for who he is and what he has done, while lament indicates that something has gone terribly wrong.

Psalm 22 is a psalm of lament. It begins with words echoed centuries later by Jesus Christ as he gave up his life on the cross: "My God, my God, why have you forsaken me?" In the midst of pain, the writer of Psalm 22 feels like God is nowhere to be found. In Psalm 23, on the other hand, we see a song of comfort and assurance, as the psalmist recognizes his God walking with him through the darkest valley. Finally, Psalm 24 is a song of pure praise. The psalmist rejoices in the King of glory, his Savior who bestows blessings upon his people.

Read It

Key Psalms to Read

For this session, read Psalms 22, 23, and 24.

Optional Reading

Read Psalms 113–118, a special collection of short psalms called Hallel ("Praise"), which is traditionally recited and/or sung during Passover.

In John 12:13, as Jesus entered Jerusalem with the crowds gathering to celebrate the Passover, they shouted, "Hosanna [O, Save]! Blessed is he who comes in the name of the LORD!" This is a direct quote of the Hallel Psalm 118:25–26. Just after Jesus and his disciples concluded their Passover meal (the Last Supper) and before they went out to the Mount of Olives, Mathew tells us "they had sung a hymn" (Matt. 26:30). This may have been the Hallel. Psalm 118 takes on new and deeper meaning, when we realize that it may have been the last song from Jesus's lips before he took up the cross.

"The LORD is my shepherd, I lack nothing. He makes me lie down in green pastures."

PSALM 23:1–2

Know It

1. How would you summarize the thoughts and feelings of the writer of Psalm 22?

2. In Psalm 23, what actions does the shepherd take to provide his sheep with everything they need?

3. List at least three ways the "King of Glory" is described in Psalm 24.

Lament and Praise

About two-thirds of the psalms express lament, while one-third are songs entirely of praise or thanksgiving. While there is certainly variation in style, lament and praise songs normally include specific elements and follow set patterns.

Laments

Lament psalms can be individual, personal prayers (examples: Psalms 13, 22, 31, 42, 43, 57, 139) or community prayers to Yahweh (examples: Psalms 12, 44, 80, 85, 90, 94). Lament songs express faith in the middle of conflict and usually:

- **address God**—making an initial plea and calling him to intervene;

- **present a complaint**—describing a problem and sometimes claiming innocence, confessing sin, or condemning enemies;

- **affirm trust**—shifting the focus away from the problem and to God who can solve the problem;

- **petition**—specifically asking God to do something (often words like *save* or *deliver* are used in this section); and

- **worship and praise**—concluding with a final word acknowledging God's faithfulness and reaffirming the psalmist's trust in God.

Praises

Praise songs include a great variety of experiences. Some praise God as the one who rules over Israel and over all things, while others focus on Jerusalem (Zion) as the sacred place where God reigns. Praise songs expound on the beauty of creation and reveal how God changed life on earth for the better by intervening in specific ways.

Praise psalms can focus on God's character or God's actions, or a mix of both, but they normally include:

- **a call to worship**—using an imperative command to praise or remember a specific action by God;

- **a reason for praise**—God's deliverance, power, or activity is described, or his character is revealed; and

- **a reprise**—a renewed call to worship and final cry of thanksgiving and praise is offered up to God.

Messianic Psalms

Many of the psalms point toward Jesus as the promised Messiah for Israel and the redeemer for all humanity. These psalms are called Messianic psalms. Psalm 22, in addition to being a psalm of lament, is widely considered a Messianic psalm.

While each psalm rose from an occasion in the life of a particular songwriter, the Holy Spirit also inspired the psalms as a witness to Jesus. New Testament writers freely draw from the book of Psalms to demonstrate how the words apply to Jesus, especially Psalms 2, 16, 22, 69, and 110, the most quoted psalms in the New Testament. In fact, Psalm 110:1 is the most quoted Old Testament verse in the New Testament.

PROPHECY IN PSALMS	FULFILLMENT IN JESUS
"Why do the nations conspire and the peoples plot in vain? ... Rulers band together against the Lord and his anointed" (Ps. 2:1–2).	Rulers conspired together to crucify Jesus (Acts 4:25–28).
"You will not abandon me to the realm of the dead" (Ps. 16:10).	God raised Jesus from the dead (Acts 2:24–34).
"My God, my God, why have you forsaken me?" (Ps. 22:1).	Jesus said these same words while on the cross (Mark 15:34).
"My mouth is dried up like a potsherd" (Ps. 22:15).	Jesus thirsted during his crucifixion (John 19:28).
"They divide my clothes among them and cast lots for my garment" (Ps. 22:18).	While Jesus was on the cross, the soldiers divided his garments (John 19:23–24).
"Into your hands I commit my spirit" (Ps. 31:5).	These were some of Jesus's last words on the cross (Luke 23:46).
"Zeal for your house consumes me" (Ps 69:9).	Jesus drove merchants out of the temple for corrupting God's house (John 2:14–17).
"They put gall in my food and gave me vinegar for my thirst" (Ps. 69:21).	Soldiers at Jesus's crucifixion offered him wine vinegar mixed with gall (Matt. 27:34; John 19:29).
"Sit at my right hand until I make your enemies a footstool" (Ps. 110:1).	God made Jesus Lord of all (Matt. 22:41–46; Acts 2:34–36; 7:56).
"You are a priest forever, in the order of Melchizedek" (Ps. 110:4).	Jesus is our High Priest for eternity (Heb. 5:1-6; 7:15–17).
"The stone the builders rejected has become the cornerstone" (Ps. 118:22).	Jesus is the chief cornerstone rejected by unbelievers (Eph. 2:20; 1 Peter 2:6–7).

Sheep and Shepherds

Caring for sheep and herd animals has been a human occupation for thousands of years. David was famously a shepherd before becoming king of Israel, and the image of a shepherd as a leader has been used by ancient Egyptian and Greco-Roman cultures, in addition to Jewish and Christian traditions.

In Psalm 23, the shepherd ensures that his flock lacks nothing by leading, feeding, and protecting them. Sheep depend on a caregiver, forming a bond with their shepherd who patiently and consistently provides for their needs.

Here are a few ways the images of sheep and shepherd are described in Psalm 23:

- **Green Pastures (verse 2):** Nomadic shepherds move with their flocks in different seasons to find good grazing land. In dry seasons, finding green grass depends on the shepherd's insight and leadership.

- **Quiet Waters (verse 2):** Sheep normally steer clear of swift-moving rivers or streams because they are poor swimmers. Shepherds lead them to calmer waters or fence off streams to create quieter places for them to drink.

- **Right Paths (verse 3):** Shepherds may work together to care for their flocks, but individual shepherds usually lead their sheep along their own pathways.

- **Rod and Staff (verse 4):** Shepherds use the curved edge of their staff as a hook to pick up sheep that may be in danger and the long shaft as a weapon to protect sheep from predators.

- **Oil (verse 5):** Shepherds may use oil to protect a sheep's nose, ears, and face from pests or infection and also as an ointment for wounds or scrapes.

The Eastern Gate

Some scholars believe that David wrote Psalm 24 after bringing the ark of the covenant into Jerusalem. Second Samuel 5–7 tells the story, and then it is retold in 1 Chronicles 16–17.

Many towns in the land of Canaan were captured, burned, rebuilt, and captured again repeatedly—but not Jerusalem. It was a city so well positioned and defended that the Jebusites who lived there claimed that a blind man could defend its walls. But then David arrived and conquered the unconquerable city. He enlarged Jerusalem and made it his new capital.

Sometime later, David brought the ark of the covenant into Jerusalem and set up a tent around it on a flat area of ground up on a high point of the city on the hill of Mount Zion. The ark was a beautiful piece of furniture, a chest decorated with angels on top and overlaid with gold. But it was more than furniture; it represented the presence of God among his people and God's faithfulness to his promises. At times, God's presence would hover just above the ark.

As the ark entered Jerusalem, the people sang and worshiped. They played music and offered sacrifices, while David danced with all of his energy before the Lord. It was an exuberant display of joy in the presence of God.

"Lift up your heads, you gates; lift them up, you ancient doors, that the King of glory may come in. Who is he, this King of glory? The LORD Almighty—he is the King of glory."

PSALM 24:9–10

Today, there is a gate in Jerusalem's Temple Mount that is bricked over. No one can pass through it. It is this Eastern Gate that would have been closest to the temple, facing the Mount of Olives. According to Jewish tradition, the Messiah will pass through the Eastern Gate when he enters Jerusalem. When the Ottoman's conquered Jerusalem in 1516, in order to prevent any observant Jew (or Messiah) from passing through that gate, they turned the ground outside of the gate into a graveyard, making it ceremonially unclean.

No bricks or graves can stop our Lord. The earth is his and everything in it. No one is worthy to stand on his holy mountain, but he makes us worthy; he makes the unclean holy (Ps. 24:3–4). When Jesus returns to establish his reign and kingdom, he will pass through any gate he chooses.

No barrier in your life is strong enough to keep Jesus out. No mistake or failure holds back his presence and love. There is nothing we can do to earn the right to stand on his holy mountain. We only believe. By trusting in Jesus—in his life, death, and resurrection—Jesus steps into our lives with new life, freedom, and forgiveness.

Golden Gate on the east wall of the Temple Mount

Live It

I Heard the Bells on Christmas Day

In 1861, Henry Wadsworth Longfellow's wife died from burns sustained when her dress accidentally caught fire. Longfellow tried to save her and was wounded so badly from the flames that he could not attend her funeral. He sank into a deep depression.

As the American Civil War began, Longfellow's son enlisted in the fight against slavery. In 1863, he was terribly wounded in battle. His body and soul were broken by the horrors of that brutal war. Longfellow went to his son in the hospital to try to bring him back to health. It was in that setting and frame of mind that Longfellow wrote on Christmas Day in 1863:

I heard the bells on Christmas Day
Their old familiar carols play,
And wild and sweet
The words repeat
Of peace on earth, good-will to men!

And in despair I bowed my head;
"There is no peace on earth," I said;
"For hate is strong
And mocks the song
Of peace on earth, good-will to men!"

Then pealed the bells more loud and deep:
"God is not dead; nor doth He sleep;
The Wrong shall fail,
The Right prevail,
With peace on earth, good-will to men."

We follow our Shepherd along the right paths, whether in green pastures with quiet streams or through the darkest valleys. Our Shepherd always leads, protects, and cares for us. Our Shepherd will prevail!

Life Application Questions

1. Why is lament—not just praise—an important part of our spiritual lives?

2. Walking on "right paths" (Ps. 23:3) can include green pastures and quiet waters, but also dark valleys. How have you experienced this in your own life?

3. What lines of lament in Psalm 22 do you most identify with—and why?

4. When you read Psalm 22, a Messianic psalm, what does it mean for you that Jesus personally understands your experience of suffering, pain, and confusion?

5. When you remember that Jesus is the King both now and in the future, how does your perspective change?

6. Write your own single-line prayer to God, perhaps something like, "Lord, what are you teaching me?" or "God, give me insight." Make this your prayer throughout the day.

My prayer:

_____.

Your Song

Compose your own prayer-song from Psalm 23 to reflect your life and to express you heart to God.

The Lord is my shepherd ...

_____

_____

_____

_____

_____

_____

_____

_____

_____

_____

_____

UNFAILING LOVE

Psalms 32 and 51

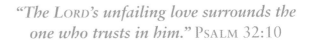

"The LORD's unfailing love surrounds the one who trusts in him." PSALM 32:10

Penitential psalms are a special category of lament that involve confessing sin and receiving forgiveness. Psalms 32 and 51 are penitential songs of human failure and divine forgiveness.

In the Jewish tradition, Psalm 32 is read on the annual Day of Atonement (Yom Kippur), along with Psalms 23 and 90. In the Christian tradition, Psalm 51 is used in church lectionaries on Ash Wednesday, a day for repentance and recognition of our weaknesses.

Guilt and forgiveness are essential parts of the Christian life, and these prayer-songs help us realize and express our own shortcomings while also receiving and embracing forgiveness from God. Every time we harm another person, we also create an offense against God. And each time God forgives us, it is more evidence of his unfailing love. When we choose the difficult path of forgiving others, we are reflecting God's character and love.

Read It

Key Psalms to Read

For this session, read Psalm 51 which King David composed after being confronted with his sins of adultery and murder; and then read Psalm 32 which also explores the themes of sin and forgiveness.

Optional Reading

For the backstory that informs these two psalms, read 2 Samuel 11:1–12:25.

You may also want to read Psalm 90, a plea by Moses for God to be merciful to sinful people.

> "Wash away all my iniquity and cleanse me from my sin."
>
> **PSALM 51:2**

Know It

1. Look at the imagery David uses in Psalm 32:3–4 to describe the anguish of keeping his sin unconfessed. What imagery or metaphors would you use to describe the burden of secret sin?

2. What does David request from God in Psalm 51? (Hint: find the action verbs that David uses in his plea.)

3. Identify all the uses of personal pronouns in these two psalms: *I, me, my, you,* and *your.* Consider underlining, circling, or highlighting them. What does this tell you about the nature of sin and forgiveness?

Explore It

Hesed

The Hebrew word *hesed* is one of the most important words in the Old Testament, and in the book of Psalms. This word is translated as love, mercy, steadfast love, loyal love, kindness, lovingkindness, faithful love, and other similar words. *Hesed* appears 245 times in the Old Testament, including 127 times in the psalms. In Psalm 136, this word is used 26 times to describe God's character: "His love endures forever." It is a beautiful and strong word that indicates loyalty and faithfulness within a covenant relationship of love. It is an essential description of God's character and is the primary motivation for the good and faithful actions that God's people experience from him. *Hesed* is love that makes and keeps promises.

You've probably known a promise of love that has been broken or fell short of what you expected. God's love is not like that.

- God promised Abraham, not only a child and a nation, but also another child who would one day come from that nation. That child would bless all people from every nation. Abraham became the founder of the Jewish people and waited for God's promise to be fulfilled.

- God promised David a child to reign over his kingdom and a ruler from his dynasty who would one day reign over a kingdom that would never end. David waited for that promise to be fulfilled.

God sent his promise to his people through prophets, poets, and leaders to declare that:

 A King would come to bring justice,

 A High Priest to offer one Sacrifice to end all sacrifices, and

 A Prophet to speak and demonstrate God's character completely.

He would bring comfort and peace to all people by laying down his own life. Then God's people waited and believed. God demonstrated his love and kept his promise by sending his Son into our world to be that Prophet, Priest, and King—and Sacrifice.

God is good to us because of who he is, not because of what we can do for him or how we can manipulate him. His faithful love for us knows no ends and no limits. In Psalm 51, God's unfailing love is the basis for forgiveness—not the sincerity of the psalmist's confession, the depth of his remorse, or the boldness of his amends. God shows mercy because of his *hesed*.

Imprecatory Psalms

More than a dozen or so psalms include statements crying out for justice and revenge against enemies. These are called imprecatory psalms. Psalm 109 is an example of an imprecatory psalm. It is the longest and most detailed in its description of vengeance, with words like: "May his days be few; may another take his place of leadership. May his children be fatherless and his wife a widow. May his children be wandering beggars; may they be driven from their ruined homes" (verses 8–10).

Knowing how to interpret and apply these psalms poses a significant challenge for Bible readers. The teachings of Jesus—for instance, "Blessed are those who are persecuted because of righteousness, for theirs is the kingdom of heaven.… I tell you, do not resist an evil person. If anyone slaps you on the right cheek, turn to them the other cheek also" (Matt. 5:10, 39)—seem to be the complete opposite of Psalm 109 in which the psalmist begs God to exact a terrible price.

What do we do with these imprecatory psalms? Here are a few things to consider:

- Revenge is not for us to exact from others, but we should be interested in standing against injustice.

- God cares deeply for justice and will avenge wrongdoing. The clear teaching of Scripture reveals, "Do not repay anyone evil for evil.… Do not take revenge, my dear friends, but leave room for God's wrath, for it is written: 'It is mine to avenge; I will repay,' says the Lord" (Rom. 12:17, 19 quoting Deut. 32:35).

- We need a safe place to fully express the pain of our deepest wounds and cry out for justice. Our heavenly Father's ears are that safe place for anything we need to say. God is big enough to handle our honesty. Don't be afraid to open your heart to God and tell him exactly what you're thinking and feeling.

- Consider the difference the life, death, and resurrection of Jesus makes regarding psalms that cry out for justice and revenge. Jesus experienced the greatest injustice, being falsely accused, betrayed, and murdered. He stands forever with those who have been treated unfairly, and he proved his vindication by rising from the dead. Jesus will take the throne of this world and establish a kingdom bringing about justice.

Live It

Come Thou Fount of Every Blessing

Robert Robinson was born in Norfolk, England, in 1735. At the age of eight, his father died, and his family fell into hard times financially. By age thirteen, he was apprenticed to a barber and sent from the country to live in the city of London. As a teenager with all the temptations of a new place, Robinson began a wild sort of lifestyle. One evening with a gang of his drunken friends, he attended a gathering where the evangelist George Whitfield was preaching. Their intention was to heckle the audience, but Robinson listened and began to change.

After investing time to explore the Christian faith, Robinson trusted in Jesus. Soon, he began to preach and was called to pastor a church. His ministry flourished, and his church in Cambridge grew over the years while he served there faithfully.

His story becomes a little more muddled at the end of his pastoral ministry, as his life came to a close. Robinson seems to have made serious mistakes in life that drew him away from faith and robbed him of joy. There are some indications that he may have been attracted by theological errors and doubts about the authenticity of Christianity.

One often-repeated story is about a time when Robinson was riding in a coach as another passenger was eagerly reading a book. He struck up a conversation with her and learned that she was reading a religious book. She shared part of what she was so excited to read. It was words that he had written many years earlier as a young Christian pastor, words that became the hymn "Come Thou Fount of Every Blessing."

Whatever the specific details of his life, Robinson understood the reality of the words he had written:

> *O to grace how great a debtor*
> *Daily I'm constrained to be!*
> *Let thy goodness like a fetter,*
> *Bind my wandering heart to thee.*
>
> *Prone to wander, Lord I feel it.*
> *Prone to leave the God I love.*
> *Here's my heart, O take and seal it.*
> *Seal it for Thy courts above.*

Yes, we may be prone to wander. However far we wander, God's grace can still reach us. If God left heaven's throne to choose death on a cross for us, there is no distance too great for him. Wherever we are, whatever we must face, forgiveness is still available from Jesus.

Life Application Questions

1. When have you felt truly and fully forgiven? And when have you truly and fully forgiven someone else?

2. Why are offenses against other people also offenses against God himself?

3. What part does confession play in the process of forgiveness? Do you think confession is necessary for forgiveness?

4. The first line of Robinson's hymn is "Come Thou fount of every blessing, tune my heart to sing your praise." How have you seen God's love tune your heart, or the heart of someone you know, over the years?

5. In Psalm 51, David expresses his determination to offer his repentant heart and life as a sacrifice. How might you offer a "sacrifice" to God today as a demonstration of repentance?

6. Is there someone you need to forgive or someone you've wronged and need to make amends with? Write out that person's name, the specific hurt and wrong committed, and what needs to happen to facilitate forgiveness.

Your Song

Compose your own prayer-song from Psalm 51 to match your life and express you heart to God.

Have mercy on me, O God ...

_____

_____

_____

_____

_____

_____

_____

_____

_____

_____

_____

Notes

HEAVEN'S ARMIES

Psalms 46 and 100

Heaven's Armies

"God is our refuge and strength, an ever-present help in trouble." PSALM 46:1

In Psalm 100:1, God calls all to worship: "Shout for joy to the LORD." Some Bibles translate this as, "Make a joyful noise to the LORD." The Hebrew word *rw'* has a fairly broad range of meaning and can refer to a shout or noise for rallying troops to battle, signaling orders, indicating victory, or praising and worshiping.

Second Chronicles 20:1–29 records an incident in Israel's history that combines the sounds of war with the sounds of praise. Jehoshaphat was king in the land of Judah when several kingdoms united for war against God's people. The king was terrified. He entered the temple and prayed, revealing the entire situation to God. Through a prophet, God gave Jehoshaphat assurance of a great victory. After that message, the temple choir rose up to praise God with "a very loud shout" (verse 19).

The next day, Jehoshaphat led his army out to meet the enemy. Marching in front was a choir singing, "Give thanks to the LORD, for his love endures forever" (verse 21). As the choir sang, God caused the enemy armies to fight among themselves. By the time the people of Judah arrived on the battlefield, their enemies had already defeated each other!

Read It

Key Psalms to Read

For this session, read Psalm 100, a song of pure thanksgiving, along with Psalm 46 which focuses on Jerusalem as the special place where God is present.

Optional Reading

Read 2 Kings 18:1–19:37 that describes a situation where the city of Jerusalem was under desperate threat.

"The LORD of Heaven's Armies is here among us; the God of Israel is our fortress."

PSALM 46:11 NLT

Know It

1. In Psalm 46, what do you notice about ...

God: _____

People (you): _____

Our world: _____

2. Identify every word in Psalm 46 that indicates safety and security (for example, *refuge, strength*, etc.).

3. In Psalm 100, what reasons are given for shouting for joy?

A River in Zion

In the eighth century before Christ, the city of Jerusalem and Judah's King Hezekiah were in a tight spot. The armies of the Assyrian Empire swept through the Middle East, conquering and brutalizing all the people in their path. They came to the city of Jerusalem and established a blockade and siege. The story is told in 2 Kings 18–19 and 2 Chronicles 32, as well as parts of Isaiah and Micah. In Isaiah, Jerusalem is described as a tiny hut in the middle of cucumber field, entirely surrounded (Isa. 1:8).

Jerusalem, unlike many other great cities, was not built on a river. The water supply came from the Gihon Spring just outside the city in the Kidron Valley. Hezekiah knew the Assyrians were coming and that lack of water would make Jerusalem impossible to defend in a long blockade. So he devised a creative solution. Two teams of workers began tunneling toward one another beneath Jerusalem.

Kidron Valley

The first team started under the city where a deep well had been dug; the second began at the Gihon Spring and worked toward the city. They cut their working time in half by meeting one another in the middle. Once the project was complete, the underground cistern filled with water from the spring, the upper spring was covered up and hidden from the Assyrians, and Jerusalem now had a stable water supply—a hidden river that would provide life-giving water even when surrounded by enemies. On the surface, there was no water, no river, but deep below the ground was a hidden spring of life.

Entrance to the Gihon Spring (illustration by David Roberts, 1842)

Sennacherib of Assyria sent a threatening message to King Hezekiah, who took the message and spread it out before the Lord in the temple and asked God to show his faithfulness. The next morning, the inhabitants of Jerusalem woke up to find their city surrounded by dead bodies: 185,000 Assyrian troops had been killed in the night. There was no battle, no noise. In the night, God defeated Israel's enemy and preserved the nation. Sennacherib returned to Assyria with his remaining troops and soon became the victim of a coup, being murdered by his own children.

There was a greater ruler than Sennacherib: God exalted over all, the one who is our refuge giving us strength, our river giving us life, so that we will not fear or fall, and so that we can be still in his presence and glory.

Be Still and Know

The striking command in Psalm 46:10 arrests us with its demanding language: "Be still, and know that I am God." This imperative word, translated as "be still," means to "leave off, be quiet, cease from striving." The Lord calls us to stop our own striving and move toward active belief. It is not a call to do nothing and just sit around all day in laziness. Being still is hard work.

In *Making All Things New*, Henri Nouwen writes:

> As soon as we are alone ... inner chaos opens up in us. This chaos can be so disturbing and so confusing that we can hardly wait to get busy again. Entering a private room and shutting the door, therefore, does not mean that we immediately shut out all our inner doubts, anxieties, fears, bad memories, unresolved conflicts, angry feelings and impulsive desires. On the contrary, when we have removed our outer distraction, we often find that our inner distraction manifest themselves to us in full force. We often use the outer distractions to shield ourselves from the interior noises.

Thanksgiving

Todah is the Hebrew word often translated as "thanksgiving" or "thanks." It appears twelve times in the book of Psalms, sometimes in inscriptions and titles, and other times within the songs themselves. This word also describes a particular temple sacrifice offered up to God out of gratitude (Lev. 7:12–15; Ps. 116:17). During the time when the Jewish people returned from exile and reestablished worship in Jerusalem, Nehemiah describes a choir that was called the "thanksgiving choir" (Neh. 12:27–47).

Being still can offer us new insights about ourselves and new opportunities to put our faith in God. Psalm 46 shows us at least three ways that stillness incites faith.

1. **Believe in God's person.**
   Being still precedes knowing that he is God. It is in our stillness that we recognize "There is a God, and I'm not him." When we are still, we recognize that he is God.

2. **Believe in God's plan.**
   At the end of Psalm 46, God has worked through judgment to bring about peace. He has worked in strange and unusual ways to be exalted. God works in even the most painful of our mistakes and through our deepest wounds to glorify himself and be at work for our good.

3. **Believe in God's presence.**
   God is present with us in completely reliable ways, even when we do not see him or feel him, even when we do not understand what he is up to or how he is working. God is with us. We can be still and trust in his presence.

Musical Notations

Many psalms begin with inscriptions containing what appear to be titles or musical directions, and some psalms contain musical notations within the lines themselves. These notes may have referred to specific tunes, instruments, or methods of playing music or singing, but no notations like modern musical notes have been deciphered. The structure of many psalms suggests that they were meant to be sung antiphonally, where a choir is split into two parts, or a leader begins, and a choir or congregation responds to the words the leader calls out.

The following table includes some of the more common notations found in the book of Psalms.

NOTATION	FREQUENCY	EXPLANATION
Selah	This is the most common notation, appearing seventy-one times in thirty-nine psalms.	While its exact purpose is unclear, it may indicate some type of break in the song, a repetition of the previous phrase, a drumbeat, or a musical interlude designed for reflection.
Mizmor	This word appears fifty-seven times, frequently in psalms attributed to David.	It may refer either to a stringed instrument or to a particular method for plucking strings on an instrument.
Maskil	This word appears in the superscription to fourteen Psalms.	This may be a title for psalms that offer specific instruction for life with God and faith.
Shir	This word appears in the title of thirteen psalms.	The word simply means "song."
Neginot	This word is included in seven psalms.	It seems to indicate the use of a particular stringed instrument.
Tephillah	This word appears in the title of five psalms.	Each of these five psalms is a call to prayer for repentance and confession of sin.
Miktam	This word appears in the title of four psalms, and each of these psalms is connected with David.	It means "inscription" or "engraving." These songs may have been carved into stone and used for public declaration in worship.
Gittith	This word appears in the title of three psalms.	It may indicate a specific rhythm for a dance or a particular instrument.

A Mighty Fortress Is Our God

At Wittenberg, Germany, in August 1527, the world felt like it was coming to an end. Two hundred years earlier the bubonic plague killed about half the population. Families and communities were devastated and altered for generations. And now in 1527, that plague had returned to claim more lives. People were struck by fear and grief as they struggled to respond. Martin Luther was a respected German Reformation pastor by this time, and people were looking to him for guidance.

Beyond the horrors of the plague, 1527 represented a difficult time for Luther. His friend, convert, and supporter, Leonhard Kaiser, was killed. Kaiser is mostly forgotten by history, but he was an enthusiastic evangelist for the Reformation. His preaching resulted in his arrest, followed by his execution.

During this time, Luther, also having been declared a heretic and outlaw like Kaiser, wrote to a friend, "I daily expect the death of a heretic." Luther was clearly shaken by Kaiser's martyrdom.

In the shadow of his friend's death and the plague, Luther—most likely reflecting on Psalm 46—wrote one of the great enduring hymns of faith: "A Mighty Fortress Is Our God."

> *A mighty fortress is our God,*
> *A bulwark never failing;*
> *Our helper He, amid the flood*
> *Of mortal ills prevailing.*
> *For still our ancient foe*
> *Doth seek to work his woe;*

His craft and power are great,
And armed with cruel hate,
On earth is not his equal.

Did we in our own strength confide,
Our striving would be losing,
Were not the right Man on our side,
The Man of God's own choosing.
You ask who that may be?
Christ Jesus, it is he;
Lord Sabaoth is his name,
From age to age the same,
And He must win the battle.

And though this world, with devils filled,
Should threaten to undo us,
We will not fear, for God hath willed
His truth to triumph through us.
The Prince of Darkness grim,
We tremble not for him;
His rage we can endure,
For lo! His doom is sure;
One little word shall fell him.

That word above all earthly powers
No thanks to them abideth;
The Spirit and the gifts are ours
Through him who with us sideth.
Let goods and kindred go,
This mortal life also;
The body they may kill:
God's truth abideth still;
His kingdom is forever.

"A Mighty Fortress Is Our
God," German hymnal

Life Application Questions

1. According to Psalm 46, what should be our response to knowing that God is our refuge and strength?

2. Who (or what) are believers' enemies today? How does the "Lord of Heaven's Armies" act as a fortress against these enemies?

3. Why does the psalmist praise God in Psalm 46? If you were composing a similar song, why would you praise God?

4. What anxieties, fears, or concerns challenge you right now? In what areas do you need God to be "an ever-present help" in your troubles (Ps. 46:1)?

5. Praising God is a weapon against our enemy. How could you use music and praise as a tool against the temptations and tricks of the enemy?

6. How can you create time and space in your busy schedule to be still and remember who God is? Consider these ideas:

- Setting an alarm as a reminder to pause in quiet prayer.

- Beginning and ending each day by talking with God.

- Reading a psalm in the middle of each day.

- Using the transition time between appointments or tasks to whisper a prayer to God.

- Other: _____

Your Song

Compose your own prayer-song from Psalm 46 to match your life and express you heart to God.

God is our refuge and strength ...

_____

_____

_____

_____

_____

_____

_____

_____

_____

_____

_____

_____

Notes

BLESS THE LORD

Psalm 103

Bless the Lord

"Bless the Lord, O my soul, and all that is within me, bless his holy name!"
PSALM 103:1 ESV

When we worship, we bless the Lord. We acknowledge that he is greater and that he rightly lays a claim to not just our entire life but to all of life; that he is supreme and we are not.

Worship is not a genre of music. Yes, you can find worship songs to sing, but worship is bigger than a musical style. Worship is not a feeling you get when you're at church or a buzz that carries you from one low moment to a higher point. Worship can involve an emotional response, but it is much bigger than a feeling.

Theologian Robert Webber explains: "Because God is the subject who acts upon me in worship, my participation is not reduced to verbal responses or to singing, but it is living in the pattern of the one who is revealed in worship." Our body, soul, and life take shape around who or what we worship.

When we recognize that God is greater than us, we bow before him, realizing he has laid a claim to everything that we are and have. And when we have yielded ourselves over to him, we become active to serve him with all the gifts and energy he has given us.

Read It

Key Psalm to Read

For this session, read Psalm 103 which paints a picture of life with God.

Optional Reading

Read Psalms 120–134, a special collection of short songs that were sung by pilgrims traveling to Jerusalem.

"[The LORD] satisfies your desires with good things so that your youth is renewed like the eagle's."

PSALM 103:5

Know It

1. In Psalm 103, what does the Lord *do*? (Hint: look for the action verbs.)

2. Considering David's life story in the Bible, how do you think his experiences with God may have influenced what he writes about God's character in Psalm 103?

3. What do you think it means to "fear the Lord" in verses 11, 13, and 17?

Hebrew Poetry

We often recognize poetry in the English language by rhyme and meter. When ending syllables make the same or similar sound, rhyme is established. Meter refers to a precise number of emphasized syllables that cause words to flow according to a regular pattern. Even free verse that doesn't rhyme sometimes follows a particular meter.

Poetry does not always work the same in different languages. The psalms in the Hebrew Scriptures are poetic and were meant to be sung or chanted. Hebrew poetry is not based on parallel sounds (like rhyming) but on parallel thoughts. Here are some types of parallelism found in the book of Psalms.

PARALLELISM	EXAMPLE
Synonymous The second line repeats the idea of the first in different words.	"The earth is the LORD's, and everything in it, the world, and all who live in it; for he founded it on the seas and established it on the waters." Ps. 24:1–2
Antithetic The second line contrasts the idea in the first.	"For the LORD watches over the way of the righteous, but the way of the wicked leads to destruction." Ps. 1:6
Synthetic The second line explains or expands upon the first.	"The law of the LORD is perfect, refreshing the soul. The statutes of the LORD are trustworthy, making wise the simple." Ps. 19:7

PARALLELISM	EXAMPLE
Climactic The second line completes the idea of the first.	"Ascribe to the LORD, you heavenly beings, ascribe to the LORD glory and strength." Ps. 29:1
Iterative The second line repeats the idea of the first in nearly the same words.	"Mightier than the thunder of the great waters, mightier than the breakers of the sea." Ps. 93:4

Alternate
Alternating lines repeat the same idea.
	"For as high as the heavens are above
	    the earth,
	so great is his love for those who fear him;
	as far as the east is from the west,
	so far has he removed our transgressions
	    from us."
	Ps. 103:11–12

Take another look at Psalm 103. What parallelism do you notice?

Praise as Worship and Service

Various words are used in the book of Psalms to describe the worship that God's people offer up to him: *praise, thanksgiving, shout, bless,* and others. Sometimes these words are used interchangeably, although they often communicate nuanced meanings. But behind all these words are two key ideas: bowing and serving. In Psalm 103, both of these ideas are present.

- The word used repeatedly in this psalm is *barak,* translated as "praise" or "bless" in most English Bibles (verses 1, 2, 20–22). This word carries connotations of bowing down. The root of this term indicates a kneeling posture.

- Near the end of the psalm, the word *sarat* is used to indicate service. "Yes, praise the LORD, you armies of angels who serve [*sarat*] him and do his will!" (verse 21 NLT).

- Together, these two words unite to help communicate the twin notions supporting praise to God: bowing down in worship and getting up to serve. It is not only our voices raised to sing but also our hands helping and our feet moving to show compassion to others that offer up an endless song of praise to our God.

The Southern Steps

Three times a year at the feasts of Passover, Pentecost, and Tabernacles, the ancient Israelites would travel to Jerusalem for worship. This practice continued through the days of Jesus.

One place that all of these travelers would have walked was the great staircase on the southern side of the Temple Mount, a place known now as the Southern Steps. A large portion of these steps has been preserved, and visitors can still walk up and down the staircase on steps that Jesus and his disciples would have used. The steps are unusual because of their varying sizes, with depths between one and nearly three feet, and the rises between steps anywhere from seven to ten inches.

Some scholars claim that the Psalms of Ascent (Psalms 120–134) were chanted or sung while standing on each of the wide steps. Rabbinic traditions written after the temple was destroyed indicate that this group of psalms was sung by priests standing in one of the temple courts. It's possible that these songs were used in both places, and very likely that they were chanted by pilgrims on their way to Jerusalem.

Remains of the Southern Steps

Geographic markers indicate a journey between the first Psalm of Ascent and the last. In Psalm 120, travelers begin in faraway Meshech (part of modern Russia) and Kedar (the Syrian desert). These places were dominated by gentiles, and getting to Jerusalem would have required a perilous journey. By the time one reaches Psalms 132–134, geographic markers indicate the psalmist's location in the land of Israel and then worshiping in unity with God's people in Jerusalem.

Day By Day

Lina Sandell was Swedish, lived during the 1800s, and saw the beginning of the twentieth century before her passing. Her father was a Lutheran pastor, and she was very close to him. While growing up, she spent many hours with him in his study. Over her lifetime, she composed 650 songs and hymns. Her deep expressions of faith were used throughout revivals in Sweden.

When Sandell was in her twenties, she was crossing a lake with her father, and because of an accident, her father drowned. Several years later, while processing her grief, she wrote the words of a beautiful hymn: "Day by Day."

If you've been hit by worry, fear, or trouble, take heart and listen to the first and last verses of this song:

> *Day by day and with each passing moment,*
> *Strength I find to meet my trials here.*
> *Trusting in my Father's wise bestowment,*
> *I've no cause for worry or for fear.*
> *He whose heart is kind beyond all measure,*
> *Gives unto each day what he deems best.*
> *Lovingly, its part of pain and pleasure,*
> *Mingling toil with peace and rest.*

> *Help me then, in every tribulation,*
> *so to trust thy promises, O Lord,*
> *That I lose not faith's sweet consolation*
> *Brought to me within Thy Holy Word.*
> *Help me, Lord, when toil and trouble meeting,*

E'er to take as from a father's hand,
One by one, the days, the moments fleeting,
'Till I reach the promised land. [4]

We discover God's faithfulness through every experience in life with our heavenly Father; even, and especially, in times of repentance, forgiveness, and seasons when we are exhausted. He renews our strength to face suffering and illness, and to find healing that we may experience in this life but certainly will in the life to come. Even when our life is dried up and passes like summer grass, God remains faithful (Ps. 103:15–17).

"For as high as the heavens are above the earth, so great is his love.... As a father has compassion on his children, so the LORD has compassion on those who fear him."

PSALM 103:11, 13

Life Application Questions

1. How would you summarize in a few words the kind of God the psalmist describes in Psalm 103? Do you recognize that kind of God in your life? Why or why not?

2. In each of the following areas, what is one thing you can praise the Lord for?

   His creation: _____

   _____

   His care for you: _____

   _____

   His character: _____

   _____

3. When we bless the Lord (or praise/worship) it doesn't change him—he is constant—but it changes us. How have you seen worship change you or someone you know?

4. What day-by-day needs and desires are you trusting God for?

5. Use Psalm 103 as prayer-song to your heavenly Father, and try changing the posture of your body as you worship:

- Kneel while resting your arms on a table or bed.

- Kneel while your arms are raised.

- Sit quietly and turn your palms upward in a position of receiving what God gives you or handing to him what you are holding.

6. Looking back over these six sessions, what is one thing that God has shown you through this study in the book of Psalms?

Your Song

Compose your own prayer-song from Psalm 103 to match your life and express you heart to God.

Bless the Lord, O my soul ...

_____

_____

_____

_____

_____

_____

_____

_____

_____

_____

LEADER'S GUIDE

"Encourage one another and build each other up."

1 THESSALONIANS 5:11

Leader's Guide

Congratulations! You've either decided to lead a Bible study, or you're thinking hard about it. Guess what? God does big things through small groups. When his people gather together, open his Word, and invite his Spirit to work, their lives are changed!

Do you feel intimidated yet?

Be comforted by this: even the great apostle Paul felt "in over his head" at times. When he went to Corinth to help people grasp God's truth, he admitted he was overwhelmed: "I came to you in weakness with great fear and trembling" (1 Corinthians 2:3). Later he wondered, "Who is adequate for such a task as this?" (2 Corinthians 2:16 NLT).

Feelings of inadequacy are normal; every leader has them. What's more, they're actually healthy. They keep us dependent on the Lord. It is in our times of greatest weakness that God works most powerfully. The Lord assured Paul, "My grace is sufficient for you, for my power is made perfect in weakness" (2 Corinthians 12:9).

The Goal

What is the goal of a Bible study group? Listen as the apostle Paul speaks to Christians:

- "Oh, my dear children! I feel as if I'm going through labor pains for you again, and they will continue until *Christ is fully developed in your lives*" (Galatians 4:19 NLT, emphasis added).

- "For God knew his people in advance, and he chose them *to become like his Son*" (Romans 8:29 NLT, emphasis added).

Do you see it? God's ultimate goal for us is that we would become like Jesus Christ. This means a Bible study is not about filling our heads with more information. Rather, it is about undergoing transformation. We study and apply God's truth so that it will reshape our hearts and minds, and so that over time, we will become more and more like Jesus.

Paul said, "The purpose of my instruction is that all believers would be filled with love that comes from a pure heart, a clear conscience, and genuine faith" (1 Timothy 1:5 NLT).

This isn't about trying to "master the Bible." No, we're praying that God's Word will master us, and through humble submission to its authority, we'll be changed from the inside out.

Your Role

Many group leaders experience frustration because they confuse their role with God's role. Here's the truth: God alone knows our deep hang-ups and hurts. Only he can save a soul, heal a heart, fix a life. It is God who rescues people from depression, addictions, bitterness, guilt, and shame. We Bible study leaders need to realize that *we can't do any of those things.*

So what can we do? More than we think!

- We can pray.

- We can trust God to work powerfully.

- We can obey the Spirit's promptings.

- We can prepare for group gatherings.

- We can keep showing up faithfully.

With group members:

- We can invite, remind, encourage, and love.

- We can ask good questions and then listen attentively.

- We can gently speak tough truths.

- We can celebrate with those who are happy and weep with those who are sad.

- We can call and text and let them know we've got their back.

But we can never do the things that only the Almighty can do.

- We can't play the Holy Spirit in another person's life.

- We can't be in charge of outcomes.

- We can't force God to work according to our timetables.

And one more important reminder: besides God's role and our role, group members also have a key role to play in this process. If they don't show up, prepare, or open their hearts to God's transforming truth, no life change will take place. We're not called to manipulate or shame, pressure or arm twist. We're not to blame if members don't make progress—and we don't get the credit when they do. We're mere instruments in the hands of God.

"I planted the seed, [another] watered it, but God has been making it grow. So neither the one who plants nor the one who waters is anything, but only God, who makes things grow."

1 CORINTHIANS 3:6–7

Leader Myths and Truths

Many people assume that a Bible study leader should:

- Be a Bible scholar.

- Be a dynamic communicator.

- Have a big, fancy house to meet in.

- Have it all together—no doubts, bad habits, or struggles.

These are myths—even outright lies of the enemy!

Here's the truth:

- God is looking for humble Bible students, not scholars.

- You're not signing up to give lectures, you're agreeing to facilitate discussions.

- You don't need a palace, just a place where you can have uninterrupted discussions. (Perhaps one of your group members will agree to host your study.)

- Nobody has it all together. We are all in process. We are all seeking to work out "our salvation with fear and trembling" (Philippians 2:12).

As long as your desire is that Jesus be Lord of your life, God will use you!

Some Bad Reasons to Lead a Group

- You want to wow others with your biblical knowledge.

  "Love . . . does not boast, it is not proud"
  (1 Corinthians 13:4).

- You're seeking a hidden personal gain or profit.

  "We do not peddle the word of God for profit"
  (2 Corinthians 2:17).

- You want to tell people how wrong they are.

  "Do not condemn" (Romans 2:1).

- You want to fix or rescue people.

  "It is God who works in you to will and to act"
  (Philippians 2:13).

- You're being pressured to do it.

  "Am I now trying to win the approval of
  human beings, or of God?" (Galatians 1:10).

A Few Do's

✔ Pray for your group.

Are you praying for your group members regularly? It is the most important thing a leader can do for his or her group.

✔ Ask for help.

If you're new at leading, spend time with an experienced group leader and pick his or her brain.

✔ Encourage members to prepare.

Challenge participants to read the Bible passages and the material in their study guides, and to answer and reflect on the study questions during the week prior to meeting.

✔ Discuss the group guidelines.

Go over important guidelines with your group at the first session, and again as needed if new members join the group in later sessions. See the *Group Guidelines* at the end of this leader's guide.

✔ Share the load.

Don't be a one-person show. Ask for volunteers. Let group members host the meeting, arrange for snacks, plan socials, lead group prayer times, and so forth. The old saying is true: Participants become boosters; spectators become critics.

✔ Be flexible.

If a group member shows up in crisis, it is okay to stop and take time to surround the hurting brother or sister with love. Provide a safe place for sharing. Listen and pray for his or her needs.

✔ Be kind.

Remember, there's a story—often a heart-breaking one—behind every face. This doesn't *excuse* bad or disruptive behavior on the part of group members, but it might *explain* it.

A Few Don'ts

✗ Don't "wing it."

Although these sessions are designed to require minimum preparation, read each one ahead of time. Highlight the questions you feel are especially important for your group to spend time on.

✗ Don't feel ashamed to say, "I don't know."

Disciple means "learner," not "know-it-all."

✗ Don't feel the need to "dump the truck."

You don't have to say everything you know. There is always next week. A little silence during group discussion time, that's fine. Let members wrestle with questions.

✗ Don't put members on the spot.

Invite others to share and pray, but don't pressure them. Give everyone an opportunity to participate. People will open up on their own time as they learn to trust the group.

✗ Don't go down "rabbit trails."

Be careful not to let one person dominate the time or for the discussion to go down the gossip road. At the same time, don't short-circuit those occasions when the Holy Spirit is working in your group members' lives and therefore they *need* to share a lot.

✗ Don't feel pressure to cover every question.

Better to have a robust discussion of four questions than a superficial conversation of ten.

✗ Don't go long.

Encourage good discussion, but don't be afraid to "rope 'em back in" when needed. Start and end on time. If you do this from the beginning, you'll avoid the tendency of group members to arrive later and later as the season goes on.

How to Use This Study Guide

Many group members have busy lives—dealing with long work hours, childcare, and a host of other obligations. These sessions are designed to be as simple and straightforward as possible to fit into a busy schedule. Nevertheless, encourage group members to set aside some time during the week (even if it's only a little) to pray, read the key Bible passage, and respond to questions in this study guide. This will make the group discussion and experience much more rewarding for everyone.

Each session contains four parts.

Read It

The *Key Bible Passage* is the portion of Scripture everyone should read during the week before the group meeting. The group can read it together at the beginning of the session as well.

The *Optional Reading* is for those who want to dig deeper and read lengthier Bible passages on their own during the week.

Know It

This section encourages participants to reflect on the Bible passage they've just read. Here, the goal is to interact with the biblical text and grasp what it says. (We'll get into practical application later.)

Explore It

Here group members can find background information with charts and visuals to help them understand the Bible passage and the topic more deeply. They'll move beyond the text itself and see how it connects to other parts of Scripture and the historical and cultural context.

Live It

Finally, participants will examine how God's Word connects to their lives. There are application questions for group discussion or personal reflection, practical ideas to apply what they've learned from God's Word, and a closing thought and/or prayer. (Remember, you don't have to cover all the questions or everything in this section during group time. Focus on what's most important for your group.)

Celebrate!

Here's an idea: Have a plan for celebrating your time together after the last session of this Bible study. Do something special after your gathering time, or plan a separate celebration for another time and place. Maybe someone in your group has the gift of hospitality—let them use their gifting and organize the celebration.

	30-MINUTE SESSION	60-MINUTE SESSION
READ IT	Open in prayer and read the *Key Bible Passage.* 5 minutes	Open in prayer and read the *Key Bible Passage.* 5 minutes
KNOW IT	Ask: "What stood out to you from this Bible passage?" 5 minutes	Ask: "What stood out to you from this Bible passage?" 5 minutes
EXPLORE IT	Encourage group members to read this section on their own, but don't spend group time on it. Move on to the life application questions.	Ask: "What did you find new or helpful in the *Explore It* section? What do you still have questions about?" 10 minutes
LIVE IT	Members voluntarily share their answers to 3 or 4 of the life application questions. 15 minutes	Members voluntarily share their answers to the life application questions. 25 minutes
PRAYER & CLOSING	Conclude with a brief prayer. 5 minutes	Share prayer requests and praise reports. Encourage the group to pray for each other in the coming week. Conclude with a brief prayer. 15 minutes

90-MINUTE SESSION

Open in prayer and read the *Key Bible Passage.*

5 minutes

- Ask: "What stood out to you from this Bible passage?"
- Then go over the *Know It* questions as a group.

10 minutes

- Ask: "What did you find new or helpful in the *Explore It* section? What do you still have questions about?"
- Here, the leader can add information found while preparing for the session.
- If there are questions or a worksheet in this section, go over those as a group.

20 minutes

- Members voluntarily share their answers to the life application questions.
- Wrap up this time with a closing thought or suggestions for how to put into practice in the coming week what was just learned from God's Word.

30 minutes

- Share prayer requests and praise reports.
- Members voluntarily pray during group time about the requests and praises shared.
- Encourage the group to pray for each other in the coming week.

25 minutes

Group Guidelines

This group is about discovering God's truth, supporting each other, and finding growth in our new life in Christ. To reach these goals, a group needs a few simple guidelines that everyone should follow for the group to stay healthy and for trust to develop.

1. **Everyone agrees to make group time a priority.**
   We understand that there are work, health, and family issues that come up. So if there is an emergency or schedule conflict that cannot be avoided, be sure to let someone know that you can't make it that week. This may seem like a small thing, but it makes a big difference to your other group members.

2. **What is said in the group stays in the group.**
   Accept it now: we are going to share some personal things. Therefore, the group must be a safe and confidential place to share.

3. **Don't be judgmental, even if you strongly disagree.**
   Listen first, and contribute your perspective only as needed. Remember, you don't fully know someone else's story. Take this advice from James: "Be quick to listen, slow to speak, and slow to become angry" (James 1:19).

4. **Be patient with one another.**
   We are all in process, and some of us are hurting and struggling more than others. Don't expect bad habits or attitudes to disappear overnight.

5. **Everyone participates.**
   It may take time to learn how to share, but as you develop a trust toward the other group members, take the chance.

If you struggle in any of these areas, ask God's help for growth, and ask the group to help hold you accountable. Remember, you're all growing together.

Notes

1   Katie Atkinson and Micheala Sosby, "Sounds of the Sun,"
    edited by Rob Garner. NASA's Goddard Space Flight Center,
    Greenbelt, MD, July 25, 2018; updated April 3, 2022, https://
    www.nasa.gov/feature/goddard/2018/sounds-of-the-sun.

2   Hermann Gunkel, *The Psalms: A Form-Critical Introduction.*
    Translated by T. M. Horner (Philadelphia: Fortress Press,
    1967; originally 1926); Hermann Gunkel, *An Introduction
    to the Psalms.* Completed by Joachim Begrich and translated
    by James D. Nogalski (Macon, GA: Mercer University Press,
    1988; originally 1933).

3   Claus Westermann, *The Psalms Structure, Content, and
    Message.* Translated by Ralph D. Gehrke (Minneapolis:
    Augsburg Publishing House, 1980; 1967); Claus Westermann,
    Praise and Lament in the Psalms. Translated by Keith R. Crim
    and Richard N. Soulen (Atlanta: John Knox Press, 1981;
    originally 1965).

4   Carolina Sandell, translated by A. L. Skoog, "Day by Day,"
    1865 (https://hymnary.org/text/day_by_day_and_with_each_
    passing_moment).

ROSE VISUAL BIBLE STUDIES

6-Session Study Guides for Personal or Group Use

THE BOOK OF JAMES
Find out how to cultivate a living faith through six tests of faith.

THE ARMOR OF GOD
Dig deep into Ephesians 6 and learn the meaning of each piece of the armor.

JOURNEY TO THE RESURRECTION
Renew your heart and mind as you engage in spiritual practices. Perfect for Easter.

THE TWELVE DISCIPLES
Learn about the twelve men Jesus chose to be his disciples.

WOMEN OF THE BIBLE: OLD TESTAMENT
Journey through six inspiring stories of women of courage and wisdom.

THE LORD'S PRAYER
Deepen your prayer life with the seven petitions in the Lord's Prayer.

PSALMS
Discover the wild beauty of praise.

THE TABERNACLE
Discover how each item of the tabernacle foreshadowed Jesus.

THE LIFE OF PAUL
See how the apostle Paul persevered through trials and proclaimed the gospel.

I AM
Know the seven powerful claims of Christ from the gospel of John.

PROVERBS
Gain practical, godly wisdom from the book of Proverbs.

WOMEN OF THE BIBLE: NEW TESTAMENT
See women's impact in the ministry of Jesus and the early church.

FRUIT OF THE SPIRIT
Explore the nine spiritual fruits.

www.hendricksonrose.com